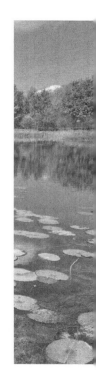

Poems By
Taylor Graham

Other books by Taylor Graham:

A Year of 13 Moons; M.A.F. Press, 1992
Casualties: search-and-rescue poems; Coal City Review, 1995
Next Exit; Cedar Hill Publications, 1999
An Hour in the Cougar's Grace; Pudding House Publications, 2000
This Morning According to Dog; Hot Pepper Press, 2001
Taylor Graham Greatest Hits 1973-2001; Pudding House Publications, 2002
Still Life with Wood Smoke; Mt Aukum Press, 2002
Lies of the Visible; Snark Publications, 2003
Harmonics; Poet's Corner Press, 2003
Living with Myth; Rattlesnake Press, 2004
Under the Shuttle, Awake; Dancing Girl Press, 2005
The Downstairs Dance Floor; Texas Review Press, 2006
Among Neighbors; Rattlesnake Press, 2007
Walking with Elihu: poems on Elihu Burritt, the Learned Blacksmith;
    Hot Pepper Press, 2010
Walking the Puppy; Lummox Press, 2013
What the Wind Says; Lummox Press, 2013

Cover Design & Illustration by Bodhi
Back cover Photograph by Heather Dana Lozano

ISBN: 978-0-9960599-9-2

Library Of Congress Control Number: 2016931080

A COLD RIVER PUBLICATION

Cold River Press
15098 Lime Kiln Road
Grass Valley, CA 95949

www.coldriverpress.com

This book could not have happened without my husband, Hatch, and the wonderful dogs who have joined us in adventure, searching for lost people, exploring the land and teaching me to observe with keener senses and fresh perspectives. Thanks also to so many poet friends, especially those in Red Fox Underground and Tuesday at Two workshops, Poem-a-Day challenges on the internet and my fellow adventurers in Medusa's Kitchen. Special thanks to Dave Boles for bringing this book to daylight.

Table of Contents

TABLE OF CONTENTS

BOOK OF HOURS

Under lava bluffs, a meadow
so delicate with flowers, a photo
might be mistaken
for a Persian rug. My photos faded
but there's memory of
a whiff of carrot – Queen Anne's lace
among the blooms untaken.
Who would pluck
a lupine from such a show?
Paintbrush in seven shades of lemon
rainbowed through the reds
to purple – this earthly heaven is
the pot of gold.
And then I'd load my dog
in the car at end of day, our time-
sheet filled as if this
were a job and, for my pay,
colors shifting in the rearview;
eastwind scraping granite
to silvertone,
and creviced ravens-rock
taking on the age-
burned luster of a burl madrone.

HOW SHE DOES IT

My dog leaps boulder to boulder,
perfect balance, not thinking where
she puts her feet. Nose to the wind,
       she factors slant of sun
and shadow, updraft, eddy, convection
off hot granite, bacterial action
on particles of scent –
              the missing boy passed
this way. She performs tightrope
math in midair, works out fluid-dynamics,
meteorology, the smell of DNA.
            I'm lost in her
universe of real-life hide-and-seek;
     I can only trust, and try to follow.
How does she do it? Instinct
to pursue, over any obstacle, one
unique scent in all the world of humans –
     answer to an equation
no computer has yet solved.
             One lost child.

ORANGE

In the dark before first-light
I slide open my dresser drawer, pull out
a cotton T-shirt. Blaze-orange
with Search-and-Rescue logo. It calls

      and from down the hall
my dog catches the scent/sound/thought-
waves/who-knows-what
in the sensory palette of dogs.
              Instantly, he's here

sniffing the fabric of old T-shirt
fresh from the wash, but still imbued
with paths through woods, crosscountry
forays up a sunburnt hill;
      he's following invisible crumb-
trails of broadcast scent, jigsaw-
pieces of what somebody smelled like,
scattered by convection and wind.

It's simple. In his chest rises
a rumble-hum wave on wave, the song
of wordless joy,
of where-will-we-go-today?

LAPSE

Memory, I mean. I mean
the pizza take-home box perched
atop the car while I loaded the important
stuff – what I'd been reading
over a combo pizza – a *carmen*, song,
a magic spell, O Fortuna. The poem
I was reading made me forget leftovers
on the roof. I drove home.
                    The pizza haunts me. Lost
forever on the road, may it become
a poem. Imagine a man in faded workjeans
wondering if he'll get supper.
And there, out of the lane
of traffic – pizza!
The crusts I was saving for my dog
he'll offer to his own,
a clever little heeler with one brown
eye, one blue, who thanks with mismatch
eyes. Behind the quick-stop
man and dog will dream in metaphor.
                    Sometimes a poem
can do this, can feed the hungry.

BORDER PATROL

Sun's behind the mountain,
sky barely dim enough to see.
It's coyote's hunting time.
I aim for the wild north corner
through rimrock, up the creek
that rips our fence out after storms –
fence we put up to keep
sheep in, danger out. My dogs
will alert me.
Loki dashes ahead, small
sable Shepherd; in faint light,
I might mistake her
for those marauders. Cowboy-
Boogie pads along
beside me, assures it's safe
to let the sheep out
with the newborn lamb
no older than the one we lost
last year to coyotes – those aliens
who lived here
long before we came.

SHEEP QUEST

They've wandered bleating
down the hall. Do they think we keep
green Spring in the cupboards
where nothing grows?

Front door to sofa – looking everywhere –
it might be in the bedroom,
purple-vetch tucked lacy in a drawer,
sweet clover beneath a pillow.

Or are they searching for lambs
under the bed, the old ewe
in a steamer trunk? She's already
made her passage.

Silence advances and the lamb
has flown
with the owl. What secrets
do we keep in our human house?

BIRD I NEVER SAW IN DAYLIGHT

It hit the windshield, changed parabola
of flight.　　　You braked the car,
ran back.
　　　　　Great horned owl broken
in the ditch. Quite dead.

How gently you cradled it
to the trunk. How many lambs like ours

disappeared to its talons.
　　　　　　　Such a beauty.
You folded it in plastic,
to ship to the museum.

　　　Now our windshield
begins its fine-calligraphy fault-
　　　　　line, a glass

trajectory of dawn-dim into bright.
　　　　Inside the Hall of Ornithology

　　　Owl stares down
from its beaked　　mask,
　　　　fixed forever-eyes, its voided
breast and fluted bones
　　　　　　　immobilized in flight.

FOX

In spring-green landscape cut by asphalt,
I walked booted on one side;
on the other, fox.
                I with my projects.

Lupine on the loose, blue sky
April breezing, oaks leaf-bursting.
Quietly a fox.

Inevitable spark when fox eyes meet human –
not love. Not terror.
                Morning belongs to fox.

At my feet, her kits slipped
into roadside culvert, their tiny house –
out-of-sight gone.

A kind of sword
cleaves the garden myth, makes a new one
in both our minds. Man/Fox.

Listen!
No matter how cautiously I step, a twig
breaks.

My home a partial paradise, between.
Stunty-oak, rimrock
                alive with hawk, lizard, fox.

ST. FRANCIS AT THE DOOR

Still dark. Coffee's perking. Black cat Blink
weaves purr around my ankles, he wants food.
 Loki dashes out the front door
then back-flash to her puppies, who hum and mewl
in the closet.
 Old dog Cowboy rolls on his back,
four feet waving his idea of yoga-pose.
 Sheep bedded down, dreaming of gates
opening to daylight pasture.

I pour myself a cup of coffee black
as sounds of creatures coming in from the dark.
 A knock at the door.
A stranger garbed in dusk. It's Francis.
He must be hungry, wandering in poverty.
He nods thanks for a cup of brew,
sits on the floor.
 Blink leaps on his shoulder.

 Can you hear him? the saint asks.
Your sheep bid you meditate – ruminate,
in your terms. Sit down, low. Let Earth speak
with the words of that puppy-choir
in the closet.
 How shall we feed God's creatures?
You know what poetry's for.

UPLIFT

Wind in the canopy of trees at trailhead,
duet with dog song of a wander-day – ordinary
summer Monday. I've got my map and daypack,
Woodsy-Owl litterbags,
                    we're wilderness-patrolling
up through lodgepole, timberline; granite and lava,
whole histories of uplift and erosion underfoot;
route of creaking wagons; the same vista
some long-ago scout tipped his hat to. Did he
feel trail-tipsy too, this
oxygen-thin high of the Sierra?

Over the saddle, down to a lake; pick up
hikers' litter – rusty can, skillet with no handle,
it all goes on my shoulders or in my dog's
saddlebags.
                    She'll swim in the lake
like snowmelt's going out of style. I'll pull off
boots and socks, let my feet flow free.
                    At last we'll hike back
under the Sentinels, eminent old men
of avalanche and thunder, vengeance of time
against stone. Who wins? We do.
We're on the trail this summer workday. Call it
                    holiday, a holy day.

BY THE ROADSIDE
Altiplano Chihuahuense

In that baked-hard landscape,
alongside the road we spotted a ramada –
the only shade for miles.
Deserted, but for the man tending *carnitas*
over a firepit, his wife ladling *frijoles* from a pot.

      There was a tiny yellow kitten
they called Milagro – a miracle
she could move at all, legs cocked at angles
never meant for walking. On scabbed
elbows she crawled over the swept-dirt floor.

Then, from scant ramada shade
she leaped,
a shaft of upbound light
to catch a moth, or simply her wish
for wings, for flight.

CALDERA

At a siphon-creek with its pond of tadpoles
and swaying grasses, we called
our dogs back from sniffing the reeking damps,
loaded into the truck and kept climbing
mesa-country; took an unmarked washboard
road. Platitudes of our travels:
        go invisible as wind; camp on the edge
of a place without a name; pack up at dawn
and leave no trace, not even fire-pit ashes.
           That night it snowed.
Hyakutake parked above us, shining his
comet headlight
down from a blacktop sky
spitting flaky white.
        After midnight, La Llorona stumbled
into my dream and slumped so cold
against the tent, I let her have my sleeping bag.
Our dogs snored through it, lost
in their own night visitations.
        At first light, gear stowed
in the truck, we drove back over washboard.
        Abundant time to determine which
way next. Another platitude:
        take the slow route
that doesn't show on a map; try to see what
nobody thought to mention.

WILD

Mini-cougar in domestic guise,
the cat assumes his Crescent Moon pose,

a motionless dance. You hardly notice
how he segues into Extended Sphinx.

He radiates indifference, a mime
of Consciousness Exhale. Claws retracted,

energy uncharted. Never mistake
it for giving up the more than possible.

The dog, who's journeyed farther with you
from the wild, lies down facing cat.

Palms reaching, Dog touches finger-tips
with Cat. Silence gaze-to-gaze.

Do you dare lie down with them,
speak to them as friends –

you with your load of expectations
in a language they don't share?

METAL-LACE

Mysterious encounters of a twilight breeze
through wrought-iron lacework – a gate
meant to keep inside and outside apart:
each with its unexpressed longings.

But this is no romance. A front-door grille
once reinforced by glass: all that separates
house-cat, never allowed outside,
from six sheep banished from a world of carpets.

Blink the cat reaches a black paw through
the grate, touches Sophie on her sheep-nose.
Freckles inches closer; her ram-child
stands non-committal watching.

The door remains latched,
sheep and cat drawn strangely together.
Evening-shadow light of eyes.

CHANGING PLACES

I hear Django in my head –
his hot-jazz singing strings, surname
of the fox – as we approach
what used to be the homeless camp,
a troupe like traveling actors
with shopping carts in place of caravan,
rehearsing ageless truths.
Shakespeare as their last venue.
The words forgotten, taken to heart.
Reinhardt playing in my head.
At the edge of oakwoods, the homeless
would smile at me and my dog
as we passed through,
before the city bulldozed them away.
Have you listened
to two-finger gypsy guitar
when it sounds like
Miranda about to meet her new
world? Wanderers
and hobos, wayfarers, romani,
where is our home?
I've lived in one place too long.

EFFIGIES

A stuffed robber hangs from that façade
on Main Street, the building
cordoned off as safety hazard, held up
by mortise-and-tenon history.
             This morning my dog leads
me under the dangling boots – dummy
accoutered now with hardhat and carpenter's
claw hammer, symbol of rehabilitation.
It hangs without fleshly odor.
My dog passes, oblivious.
          Dogs have their principles.
Mine distinguishes the neighbor girl, hiding
behind a classroom, from the scarecrow
who guards her school garden.
My dog knows, only the child is human –
            not like what he showed me
in a forest clearing, stuck in logging-
berm dust; five stick crosses in a row,
wooden bodies with stiff lashed arms, dirty
towels bound about their heads:
          father, mother, child-sized dolls
of our native lumber, lined up for target-
practice, pelleted with slugs.
They still held the scent of booted shooters
who planted them there footless:
           something out of place
in those cedar woods. Not human.
My dog moved on.

ARRANGEMENTS

This BBC recording, Perlemuter playing
Ravel, has roused the crook-tail kitten
from his flannel bed. He's found a string
to worry. The string's connected
to a flash-drive which now the kitten's
trying to unravel. It might take him
at least forty seconds to knock its memory
loose, as if struck with a hammer.
But he's bored with that. He's making
snow-angels on a stack of papers,
small seismic event that's uncovered
a poem I thought I lost. Perlemuter's playing
Ravel, *Le tombeau de Couperin*. All
of them dead now, all alive. How magical
this collaboration – arrangement in time
against time, on a winter day.

LIZARD KARMA

Morning's dim and cold as
a winter snake. It's early March –
frost on the grass, ice
on the windshield. Sun-glare coming
up over Stone Mountain. I pull off
the windshield wrap, and out
falls a lizard. It's the wrong season.
What instinct drew him
to yesterday's faded warmth
of my little Honda? Western fence-
lizard: flat skull of hope; blue
on throat and belly – vibrant blue.
My numb fingers tingle
with lizard. I hold him under jacket
and vest, I'll carry him
to the woodpile, where sun strikes
first, this time of year.
Too late. Already he's clasped
my shoulder with tiny lizard claws,
seeking heat. Inevitably
headed for my neck, climbing.
How to untangle a lizard
from collar and hair? How
disengage one life from another?

DIAMONDBACK

No daydreams
where you wind your cold
machinery.
I once
set a foot too close
and still
my knees
feel the abyss.
The canyon
shimmers your colors,
your brawny
compaction.
You're the muscle end
of a universe
where nothing but
grace
counts.
Still you advance
sleek on scales,
a coiled
spiral that never closes
but
echoes, echoes.

TRICKS OF AN OPEN WINDOW

Faint odor of skunk on the air.
You're looking through old letters

for what you never quite understood,
phrases misread, wishes hiding

in dashes and margins.
Roadkill skunk, white stripe

on centerline. You fold a letter back
in its envelope – things gone by.

What would you write the dead
of how their fair world has changed?

Elegant creature with its rakish
white scarf caught in the turning wheel.

Now alights on your papers a moth,
wings laced ebony and umber.

Perfection in the wind.
Alive. A window to let things fly.

OUR MOUSE

Catfood stashed in a coffee mug
hung from the kitchen cabinet.

In the drawer of important papers,
shredded bond and yellow insulation

pale as crocus for a nest.
Bright eye rising – a small dark sun

with tiny satellites – her babies
hanging from her teats. She slipped

up-backwards
behind the drawer half-open; babies

disappearing as they clung;
just her tail still showing, tip of tail.

I could squash them in the drawer;
leave it open for the cat.

But all these days I've fed her,
given her Easter-yellow for a nest.

Look, I've seen her eye.

VISITATION

It passes
over – El Greco
silhouette
in flight. Dark
on this gray December sky.
A great blue heron

on approach –
descent. I'm holding
breath, heart wingbeat
to land
with Heron, who now stands thin
in winter stubble,

our muddy
field. Arrow-crested;
bill-neck-legs
perfect fine-
nib penstroke. It fixes me
with its reedy eye.

A MISPLACED SHEET

shuffled by the puppy, those old files –
xeroxed forms we filled out at the end
of searches – hundreds of sheets in piles
of loss. An old man gone; sails to mend
or sink a body how many miles

from where he disappeared; a pier; send
him weighted beyond finding by dogs.
That misleading report by a friend
had us trudging through windfalls of logs;
a man still missing on mythic isles

of the not-found. Siren songs of frogs
as we called the lost names. Meadow frost
dissolving footprints like sheets of fog.
Whoever could add up all the cost?
The puppy scatters what she can't spend,

a jumble of tales and places jackstraw-tossed,
these randomly shuffled sheets of lost.

HOW TO FIND THE PLACE

At trailhead I check the ground for sign –
scuffs, arrows, footprints. My dog says *this*
way – up creek, past the waterfall,
switchbacks to a fork.

By intuition, or lift of my dog's nose,
I choose a lesser path. It promises
no view, but disappears in willow thicket
quick with warbler wings.

Here's an opening that pulls me –
not a swale, exactly, just a tease
to follow.
Feel how it draws without intent.

Two great boulders like a gate:
the sudden vista.
This is where he'd stop
to aim his camera; where he'd focus

on the world through his lens,
stepping without looking
a bit to the left, or
            to the right, for the best angle,

the spectacular shot; not seeing
the edge.

QUAKE LABYRINTH

We climbed stairs to the landing,
and a door, but it was jammed.
Another de-construct
of earthquake that knocked   down half
a building here, dissolved
some walls, left others standing, and jammed
this door.   Beyond, a long bare
corridor with countless open doors.
The secret lives of offices
past closing,   one night watchman
making his rounds. Where
did the quake   catch him?
          Pry open that jammed
door, the whole human structure
might fall down.   But a dog
is license and language of her own.
Open sesame, she wriggled
     through. Door by cor-
ridor –   a slat of light
let us watch her disappear;
back into view, diminishing, progressing
methodically room by
room through every door. At last
she came back.
No one there. So much
                    labyrinth
beyond
what was not a door.

TALAVERA

As if spilled milk glazed over native sands
hard-fired but not unbreakable –

my dog pads over porcelain no longer
ornamental, fragments of

tiles delicate blue on white, sky painted on
cloud, the world topsy-turvy

with shattered walls. Rhythmic breathing
of my dog inhaling scent

that rises through cracks from tiny cells
of space, how far beneath

what had been
corridor and room – bronchioli, alveoli

compressed as if a giant stamped
across this portion of

city, leaving fragments of lintel-rebar-bone.
But look. Someone

has set aside one tile unbroken –
as if to neaten, no,

as token of a chance to raise one
living from the dead.

ALPENGLOW

on a line by Emily Dickinson

How the old mountains drip with sunset,
she wrote, who never saw our western peaks
by alpenglow – soft carnelian stain of light
between spring-blossom and raw flesh;
the closest that bare rock comes to the color
of our lives. The first time I saw it, mid-
summer Sierra, I thought of death,
and shivered, and didn't stay to watch night
fall. I've learned to live with that complex,
fragile color washed over avalanche
that buried a man I'd never know; my dog
sniffing for scent rising carnelian from under
snow. Our lives so beautiful by alpenglow.

CONTEST

to see who could loose the gold-
line faster as the sun
slid its prusik down, across

dead dry grass in and out of live-
oak shade, August sparking
parch, sparkling sweat

from the ascent of granite.
Slick as snake-skin, click of
carabiner, friction

of cicada. As if all summer
we'd been partners suspended by
piton and belay, our lives

for the impossible
view. And then at the end,
the two of us rushing

against the dark, stuffing
red-orange-yellow
rope woven with violet, a sheath

like rattler's diamonds
into nylon bags, blue-water, sky-
line, as if the whole

adventure were to see
late afternoon in shadow
of the summit.

DOG MUSIC

Loki presents me with
a bone, then takes it back. A favorite
old bone from the butcher,
honed by her teeth. Quite hollow.
Polished, devoid of marrow.
She rolls her spine over it, and grins.
She stares as if it held
mysteries. She stares at me. *Look!*
See! The leg bone's
connected to the
knee bone. I kneel, raise it
to my eye,
gaze through. It's a monocle,
a singular spectacle,
telescope to other worlds.
Cross-section of some creature's
shank, this bone
glistening with stars. I blow
through it, exhale
breath-wind in her dog-face.
Scent music.
She has no words
but wonder.

ASPEN GROVE

Somewhere between French Camp
and Tanglefoot, my dog and I started up
the trail, climbing hairpins
through dusty hot – ceanothus, manzanita –
up to a sudden
midst of silent green community.
Family of aspen all of a root,
relations without words.
The language confusing at first.
My dog stopped in the trail,
sniffed breeze, cocked her ears.
Every aspen leaf a-tremble, origami –
if paper could be so delicate.
Skin of paper, as if
someone had written a history of snow
over rock over snow. Centerpiece
of one living tree
with so many minds; a net of roots
to hold the mountain together.
Whispers I couldn't quite hear, angels
on the breeze
of a half-moon day. My dog
stood listening. Shiver-cool of noon.

INHALE THE SKY
for old dog Cowboy

My dog's tracking our quarry – across grass
to tennis courts, along the shady treeline. Then

whoop! He cuts south, the breeze full
in my face then behind my back, hide and seek

with sky and my dog swings wide and happy.
Head high. Forget that step-by-step

trail of evidence, every wrong turn the "lost man"
made. Cowboy was born to range

unfenced give-him-land far from road give him
hills and valleys, green grass playing-field

on summer break, he's moving too fast to tell
where he's going, he intercepts scent free-

flowing on the briefest breeze. Straight
to his quarry, the wrong way, who cares?

He's old enough to be retired. To lie
at my feet and dream. Just this morning,

let him lift his nose off the ground,
inhale the sky entire.

PREEMIE

A lamb born too early; the joints
of his legs tangled clumps
ligament to bone.
He stands up
to fall, to prop himself
back up on elbows, and stand
again. His sister
gambols as lambs should.
Between sun and sparse grass,
he takes in both
in brief spurts of mother's milk.
The brown deepens
in his eyes, blood in his veins,
each hour he's a little less
transparent.
His mother moves off
half a dozen yards to better
grass – worlds away
to a lamb so tiny; leaving
him alone. He hums to himself.
He's the center
of the corner of her eye.

HOLY WELLS DAY

The overwintered pond boils with spring
ferment; depths I can't read, and
a tinge of blood churned into roadside mud.

The old dog lies guard. Yesterday he was kept
inside as the ranch-butcher did his deed,
hanging the carcass from his truck-winch,

spilling ram's blood on gravel.
An old dog feels responsible, even for that
agate-eyed skull-casque ovine

who rammed him into the fence
for being a dog. A good shepherd forgives,
but can't forget his duty.

Now, hang-dog, he lies vigilant
as his ewes and lambs step out into spring
morning to feast on filaree,

then lie meditating while their rumens
ferment the day to green wine.
Rain-washed clean, the creek runs exuberant

over rocks. Today
no monster-truck rumbles up the drive.
The old dog makes sure.

GUARDIAN

The vixen appeared as you sat
crying out a sister's loss.

This fox had no tail. She barked as if
to stir you from your dark.

What is the death of a child?
Your sister says the world's a trap,

an abandoned freezer that latches
with a snap, and no way out.

The vixen's kits are gone.
Her eyes could read Greek tragedy.

Your sister has closed
her mouth on questions about

heaven. Still, you walk
the oak woods for an answer

as the vixen shadows
you, light among lost creatures.

RIGHT NOW,

I have no frogs in my cake pans – the ones I put out
    as shallow pools
of water on my deck, where my wet-mop hangs
    after swabbing the floor.

Tiny masked brown frogs hang out in my mop, their
    ponds gone dry.
Two counties south are burning. So brittle, this cusp
    of a droughty fall.

Breeze carries oak leaves and pine needles
    to float on water
in my cake pans, so they resemble pools in the
    woods, refuge for a frog.

We cherish small water, portion it out for lizards
    and birds, and now
the frogs.

The thrift-store lady pointed to my 50-cent pans:
    Baking a cake?
They're for water, I said. The sweetest taste of all.

DANCE WITH THE DOG

I touch her paw
and bow.
May I, human, have this dance?

My wild little partner
doesn't know the steps, she's
forever knocking me

around. I swing left,
but already she's twirled across
in front to trip me.

She doesn't grasp
that two bodies (mine and hers)
can't occupy the same

space at the same time,
even dancing.
Elementary physics, a human

construct. How much
we think we know; how much
goes dancing

off beyond our understanding.
Is this how my dog
loves me, this more than

togetherness?
Maybe she's obeying laws
of a different universe.

A STRANGER'S HORSE

Sun strikes aslant a sorrel gelding
on a grassy hilltop. Retired cutting horse.
He's earned his ease, after years under spurs
and stop-watch.

I never could leap astride
without a stirrup.
I ask if he regrets the time he lost.

He lowers his head.
His whole bulk collapses onto cropped grass.
Legs in the air, knees, hocks released.

Grunting, spine-twisting
side-to-side as divots fly and the ground
shakes.

Slack-jaw, worn teeth grinning
upside-down
before he pulls his limbs
together, rights himself, hooves to turf.

I could kick off
my shoes, I could let grass grow
between my toes.

DOG POETRY

There we sat
on Main Street, hawking books of poetry.
Dog poetry. Main Street is for bead-boutiques
and tourists clicking smartphones
at Gold Rush architecture.
Poetry hangs in closets with the ghosts.
But dogs –
half the Main-Street walkers were in tow
to cockapoos, terriers, and this
some kind of mid-size dog with wild soft
hair cinched at the face by a halter.
She dove straight
between my knees, scrubbing her cheeks
against me, begging with eyes
browner than her coat of pillowy hair –
begging to be petted, saved
from this indignity, this human notion
of dog-master bond.
I tried this same
contrivance with my own dog once,
and watched him fling himself to ground
as if to rub fetters from his muzzle.
My dog, who composes poems with his nose.
I looked into this stranger's
eyes and put my face against hers, inhaled
the stories of her brown hair.

LOCO-MOTIVE

My crazy puppy, electrified
energy.
After all the systematic training
official by-the-book, brick-
boring
  she lost the nova
in her eye.
It broke my patience, keeping her close
as a bad secret.
I packed her in the truck,
headed upcountry. End of pavement,
        wild-flowers past
their prime, faded like ruined puppies;
dry stems of wild carrot, lupine
gone to pod.
              I unclipped her
leash. She leaped feet flying,
rapturous.
I called, she circled –
keeping me
in the glint of her eye –
        dashed off to scout
the rest of the endless wind-
blown world. Free as thistledown,
this dog I hadn't been sure
  I loved.

THROUGH THE FOG

Between the landing where they turn native
cedar into carbon pencils, and the wreckage
of a great madrone felled for its red burl,
I'm wandering in my fog of human blindness.
Sight is a lockbox for what little the eyes
can see. The map tells me nothing
except where I am; no X to mark the spot
we're headed, guided by my dog who's
accountable only to her nose. Here's
the confluence where inversion joins down-
draft rich with the scent of a lady who
yesterday went to pick mushrooms.
My dog's nose unravels whole narratives,
messages mailed from the Land of Lost.
Clear as if written in frost crystal: *Through*
the fog, this way. Believe your dog.

SCHAFFUNG

You sent me a German poem about sheep, *Schafe*.
And now my small flock led by Sophie the con-
artist passes my window, nibbling grass and forbs.
With clever teeth she takes a little bite (*ein Bisschen*,
like my *bisschen Deutsch*). Greens protrude from
lips fluent as fingers. And here comes Cowboy my
German Shepherd *Schäferhund* who has no thought
of herding sheep. He's reading the morning news
on a wind just arrived at the door of our landscape,
Landschaft of our outskirts of discovery. Your poem
got me thinking about *schaf's* small flock of root-
letters. Sophie my *Schaf* dislikes roots, she goes for
the succulent leaves, the flowers, the poetry – poetry
being a *Schaffung*, a creation. Pointless, trying to
reason such things out.

I'll walk outside and see
if a poem like a spring-lamb
dancing comes.

UNDER WILD PLUM TREES

It's been half a year since coyotes killed the lamb.
You walked down the swale into the dry creekbed,
up stair-step rocks that, in winter, cradle a still pool,
to the place where they left her almost intact, just
dead. So many months later, you had to hunt,
think back, remember. After half a year, no trace
of where they dragged their kill. No skull, not
a nub of wool. We never saw vultures. Other
creatures – raccoons and foxes, green-bottle flies
and beetles – must have feasted. Bacteria, fungi.
The lamb is gone, the universe is fed.
I wonder where her bleat went, her nuzzle,
the soft brown focus of her eyes.

A VENUE, A WAKE

At first light down by the creek
there sits this early morning
a judge-bird. No. Two, perched low
on the rocks. A third
vulture atop a ghost-pine.
I ease the space
between us. I want a better view,
I want to know
what brought them.
If I step too close, too fast....
One bird lifts off,
settles higher. Five, six
more in ponderosa. Another pair
in an oak that leans across
the way.
I'm losing
count. Two more sail in,
dawn shining through their wing-
fingers.
In green-
grassy swale, a departed deer,
spirit-slipped in the night,
and now fifteen undertaker-birds.
They've come
to make death clean.

GRACE

A hairsplitting instant sun-in-the-eye
blinding as I second-geared
the grade out of Weber Creek –

doe out for a stroll. No,
on skinny sprung-coil legs she made
1-2-3 quick spring-vaults

across pavement, inches from metal.
Safe on the other side.

Pensive in wonder
at how so much animal-mass
could levitate like it was natural, &

encumbered in seatbelt/harness,
I braked,
altered speed-momentum-purpose,

I was rapt, wrapped in deer-grace –
if only for the passing
moment.

APOGEE

Moon watched the fox kit
skitter across pavement while its mother-
vixen hunted up the hill.
This was a new moon, younger
than the kit, but wiser, having gone through
so many lives of changes.
It watched convergence of kit
with blinding light, more blinding
than the moon would ever be
except in lovers' eyes;
watched invisible wheels
turn the kit on two-lane centerline;
heard the mother-vixen wail – a sound
like there is no other.
But she would have other kits,
as Moon grows a-new
replacing the one gone dark.
This kit she's lost glows
fox-silhouette for oncoming drivers
to marvel at the keen
receptor-ears, the subtle nose flared
even after their headlights have passed;
still limned by moon.

CAT LIVES

The old cat weighs no more than
teeth, claws, and purr, the bones inside.

A cat is a cat: lap comfort, or
too much togetherness, Egyptian god,
mummy demanding my mind.

Tonight *I want to tell you something*
with my hands, I say. She turns
to lick her flank, her thigh, what's left

of fur after thirteen years together.
I could tabulate each vertebra

down her spine. She still knows
how to purr, as long as
hands think of pain as a flit

against the pane. The bird flies.
Feathers of bird-wings in flight, bones
inside. In her next life, in mine.

RIGHT THROUGH TOWN

The chance of a child wading across
a flooded creek: inverse to the downward
surge of upcountry rain, muddy water
teeming with tree-limbs, plastic bottles,
rope, old tires. A stenciled NO
SWIMMING sign bobbed ahead of us
as the officer guided his raft –
technique and skill to run a current
gone wild through town.
He knew his craft as I knew my dog,
who stood balanced at the Zodiac's bow.
My job, to watch for a nose-dip,
a head-turn that might prove the missing
boy's scent. Behind us, out of sight
now, two figures bent over
a votive candle at the spot where their son
disappeared. As we passed, I focused
on my dog. I didn't see them.
I can't get their faces out of my head.

SHOPPING WITH GINSBERG

Allen, you asked who killed the pork chops.
I only led the lamb to barnyard
on his way to becoming mutton. The new
moon can pass through a dark sky
and still cast shadows. Our dogs sleep
quiet till almost dawn, senses
pricked for the slightest murmur,
the ocean-ward flow of blood through veins
and out again, breath back to sky.
The lamb waits among his flock, with time
to meditate the stillness of bare
earth, the weave of wire under a glint of stars.

HIGH SPRING TIDE

Through a haze of sleep-
lessness eight puppies swim out
of her amniotic ocean, to this coast
littered with woolen remnants,
worn carpet, chair- and trouser-
legs. The newborns gasp without gills
for breath; blind as a blue moon;
their mother calling them by scent
of first milk; calling them
by names a human will never learn.
Yet each will grow
to heed a stranger's voice,
and follow it to the end of this
eroding world.

ABOVE HIDDEN LAKE

From a certain spot on the rim,
what a view – the over- and under-
worlds of peak and canyon,
plumes of smoke north and south –
wildfires sparked by lightning-strike.
West, over the valley, clouds
sticky-dark as treacle. Trail-crew
off fighting fire. I've got this blue-sky
bit of mountain to myself,
its winds. Itch of ions in the air.
We're buoyed, my dog and I,
past summer cabins, dry meadow,
above the last lodgepole.
Up here, winds rule.
Brusque from the east, then shoosh
of siphon-wind – dark twist
of cloud, stamen of storm-flower.
I imagine smoke-plumes
building pyrocumulus, boiling its own
weather. Miles from here. But
flash! to the east, thunder
follows lightning too quick for
countdown.
Better hike to lower ground,
bowing thanks to the overworld lords.

SHOW ME

In my field guide, image
of Horned Puffin, a bird I've never seen.

But loons! on a stormy Kenai summer lake,
thundering the water – not seen
so much as heard. Hard splat of waves
against canoe, our young dog on guard at the bow;
we paddled for shore, the tiniest island.

Incredible generosity of dogs, loons and lake
in a storm. The quality of light sulphur-ionic, dark
till daylight. What our earth reveals and hides.

Some mornings I wake up
feeling like a horned crone – this image
in my mirror. What do the eyes know?

Without a sound, loons still call, more haunting
than wild geese. There's a lens behind
my eye that sees what's gone, what doesn't die:
a dog looking back over her shoulder,
making sure I follow

if I'll believe, and tell her
"Show me!"

PORCH LIGHT

That night the moon was broken –
     the Poet's Moon for walking unleashed
fancies in the dark. The moon
       who moves things from their daylight
places. Moon of broken ropes
and latches. In the dark
        I saw a golden glow
from the barnyard. Our sheep were gathered
     'round the light of a Coleman lantern filched
from the shed. They sat in a circle,
     ankles crossed over shanks,
    one ram and three ewes gazing intent
at the cards they held in cloven hooves;
lambs clustered around the half-lit fringes.
     Rosy was dealing. Freckles, poker-face;
Sophie trying to peek at her cousin's hand;
     Tygh-bo inscrutable
behind his agate eyes.
     What game of cards do sheep play,
while in the dim house their masters
read the history of humanity or watch TV?
     How high are the stakes?
     How high the moon? I turned to ask,
but she was broken,
     all her fancies free to fly.

BUTTERFLY EFFECT

A lacewing lands on my palm – I might clap,
   smash it, or let it
rest and, when it wishes, fly. Shockwaves in air
   widening circles in a
pond fluid dynamics the laceflight of wings,
   or my bare hands
concussing. Listen. I've heard a single butterfly
   passing through sky
has consequences not guessed. If I write this down,
   or speak it so the free sounds fly,
what repercussions? What ringing unrhymes?
   Might someone
believe the metamorphosis of words in
metaphor, so they metastasize to
something I couldn't imagine....
What dare I
do this
day?

TERRIBLE LOVELY

Our rocky hilltop admits no owner.
Before we came, a hawk
made a stick-nest in the high crotch of an oak,
where she inculcated her fuzzy-
headed hawklet with the metal-saline taste
of songbird blood.
Towhees kept to their dark and private
brushpiles. From nest's edge,
her chick observed the world, then fledged.

Songbirds returned to daylight.
　　　　　I learned the names of winds here,
but they don't come to my call,
any more than that low-flying scream
which sometimes drones
our woods, a quick shadow wingswept
as small death, tracing paths
left by the flight of prey.

Today at dusk I surprised my hawk
among rocks – so close!
She rose and red-eye glared, then
sailed away.

I'm no more to her
　　　　　than I am to the wind.

STUDY-SKINS

This owl, for instance,
has no eyes – what had been
amber lanterns in the dark

are dead. Toe-tagged,
the talons grasp at species-name
and wingspan as if a ticket

to flight. A girl holds her
carefully penciled notes; knows
somehow she's been

scammed. It was the living bird
she loved. Royal gaze
of osprey. Vagabond journey

of a thrush caught outside
its range, its schedule.
The bird in motion – hawk

so high she can't see field-
marks; or that tiny
twitter weaving in and

out of thorn-berry tangle.
She misses
the eye of the bird.

ON A WIRE

I think of the woman clutching
branches and trunk of a tree above cycloning
waters as she gives birth to her child.

I think of the young bitch caught
ahead of schedule, delivering her puppies
in a wire shipping crate.

I listen to hum of puppies in the deep den
of closet, where their mother carried
them, not satisfied with a safe whelping box.

They're humming puppy-dreams
with full bellies; they've been pulling warm,
sweet milk from their mother

like young elephants reaching
for a leafy frond, or toddlers at breakfast –
tree-branch or cheerios,

the children will be fed. A mother
does as she must,
so much fear and famine in her joy.

ABRACADABRA WIND

In her prime, Pattycake
would run mazes of manzanita thicket,
huzzah! she'd cruise fenceless
to the next county.

One day she keeled over
sideways; jerked back on shocked legs,
shook her head, embarrassed
we'd noticed. Do dogs have strokes?

Five trips to the vet in two weeks.
          X-ray, ultrasound, state-of-the-art
flashdoodles I didn't understand, except
our old dog was dying. Fluid on the heart?

For all his words, the vet couldn't say.
                    Lacking the abracadabra,
he drained her abdomen.
We woke up Thursday – on the docket,

          another trip to the vet.
I let Patty out the door
to splendiferous morning. She ran out
the ridge a free dog. Woo-Hoo!

challenging the whole granfalloon
and especially that young bitch
down the hill.
In full ishkabibble stride

it knocked her dead. Patty was done
with vets.
I can hear her running
when the wind's just right.

LAST OF SUMMER

Swallows became small boys
concealed in the old barn's drafty
loft. No, the swallows after all these
summers were immune
to small-boy sorcery. They caught a slip-
stream off the brisk westwind
that skimmed upcanyon, intersection
of willow stringer through
the cow camp meadow, two miles
of washed-out road through encircling
forest. The foremost in our tribe
of hiders was off to college.
My old dog, once so adept at finding
him, lay by the pickup, sensing
changes. Ravens gathered notorious
in the tops of pines, raucous
with a croaky undertone of thunder
to their corvid-latin. Would it
storm? The clouds
converged. We gathered up
our wrappers, scrims of poems
from the flower-fading
of July; a bowl of leftover
words to take back down the hill
and home; each word
possibly the seed
of a coming winter's song.

GO TO THE RIVER'S EDGE

This is where someone saw
the two of them go in – the girl
on a boulder by snowmelt current,
her fiancé with camera, onshore,
gesturing for her to move
a little to the left for a better angle.
She slipped into the water.
Swept away. He
jumped in to save her. Gone,
the two of them –
flailing arms and feet, shrieks
against the torrent.
This morning my dog
ran the shoreline of river-wild,
held by a scent-thread
she wouldn't let go; whining,
gazing at that island of rocks –
do you see it?
In underwater caverns,
fairy tale lovers might live
forever, crystal cold, breathless
blue.

SHINGLE CREEK

I walked past the old homestead where once
a girl pined herself to death of loneliness, here

among the roses and dairy cows, the song of frogs
on the pond. I kept walking

and of course my dog came too. Loneliness
is incompatible with dogs.

We paused to watch an egret lift silver
from a snag and settle on the lake's far shore.

Tall spring grasses verged to summer-gray,
the woods to deeper green,

a place I'd never ventured. No trails.
My dog led the way – then stopped. Some-

thing faster flashed past us and away.
Coyote, shape-shifter of this not-quite

settled land; creature unburdened by thought
of trespass; his light of passing beyond.

THE CROW'S TALE

Softly the screen-door
after supper – sweet residue
of carrots in the roast, a bitter edge
of celery. Old man tired of words.
In the distance, some neighbor
at last-light's target practice, plink-
plink-silence-plink, a sort of
Sunday evening Morse. Old man up
the eastern hill, shadows down
behind him in the swale,
dark water in a cistern. Crows
out of treetops, wing-tips aflame
in sunset of an agate sky,
their rise and circling, bank
and swirl in figure-eights a black
equation: answer = night.
Except one crow to one old man
as if by name. What
words? What language?

FINDING ME

We left our truck in a turnout curve,
hiked up through hemlock, lodgepole,
white pine. You checked the quad-sheet
for old survey benchmarks;
recalled distinctive species of the subalpine
zone,
                while our dogs ran scouting
unfamiliar scents – wolverine?
Thin air. Decomposed granite sprinkled
with pussy-paws, mules-ears,
mariposa lily.
                  One heavyset juniper
clung to mountain by its roots; its crown
wind-scaled; lightning-scarred
all the way down to stone; the whole tree
split, hollowed by its summit-share
of storms. Hanging on.
                      Its core open,
I stepped inside; implanted
myself in juniper; looked out on the world,
over a lake I thought I knew. It seemed
more seriously blue from this
viewpoint, as if my eyes gathered
              that much more sky – Earth spinning
on the axis of this peak rooted in tree.
A thin-air dream, altitude hallucination.
                My dogs ran ecstasies
at finding me inside the compass
          of a tree.

TEN YEARS FROM NOW

the old dog will still appear in dreams,
as she has for decades.
Follow me!
she pirouettes before me,

then trots ahead into darker woods,
glancing back over her shoulder
as dogs do,
to make sure I'm coming.

She's found something
she needs to show me: a lost child;
an old woman wandering away
from her life.

A dog moves so fast
through willows, how could I keep up?
She leaps from rock to rock,
from summer creek to summit to stars.

Last night in dream the mountain
beckoned. Mariposa lilies
blooming on scree,
thunderheads over the peak.

Close my eyes, it's where I live.
So many years
since I climbed a mountain.
At last the mountain comes to me.

Taylor Graham has been a volunteer search-and-rescue dog handler for more than forty years. She and her husband, Hatch, responded with their trained German Shepherds to hundreds of missions in Alaska, Virginia, California and beyond. They are veterans of the 1985 Mexico City earthquake, the Loma Prieta earthquake and the Berkeley-Oakland Hills firestorm. While they no longer go on searches, they still train their own dogs and help others in their local training group.

Taylor spent two summers as a Forest Service volunteer ranger in the Mokelumne Wilderness, with her dog, and she's assisted Hatch - a retired forester-wildlife biologist - in some of his projects, notably the California Bluebird Recovery Program, establishing and monitoring nestbox-trails for cavity nesting birds.

Taylor earned an M.A. in Comparative Literature from the University of Southern California and spent a year in Germany on a Fulbright. Her poems have appeared in *The Iowa Review, The New York Quarterly, Poetry International, Poetry Now, Rattlesnake Review, Sacramento Voices, Southern Humanities Review, Tule Review* and elsewhere. She is included in the anthologies *California Poetry: From the Gold Rush to the Present* (Santa Clara University) and *Villanelles* (Everyman's Library). Her book *The Downstairs Dance Floor* (Texas Review Press) was awarded the Robert Phillips Poetry Chapbook Prize.

PUBLICATION CREDITS

The 2River View: Border Patrol

Bellowing Ark: Visitation

Bitterzoet: Last of Summer; Right Through Town; Under
        Wild Plum Trees

Blue Unicorn: Guardian

California Poets: Abracadabra Wind

Carquinez Poetry Review: Fox

Convergence: Lapse

Epos: Diamondback

Freshwater: Contest; The Crow's Story

Jellyfish Whispers: Bird I Never Saw in Daylight; Show Me

Manzanita: How to Find the Place

The Meadow: Changing Places; Preemie; Through the Fog

Medusa's Kitchen: Above Hidden Lake; Dance with the
        Dog; Dog Music; High Spring Tide; Inhale the
        Sky; Metal-Lace; Porch Light; Quake Labyrinth;
        Sheep Quest; Study-Skins; Terrible Lovely; Tricks
        of an Open Window; Wild

Message in a Bottle: A Misplaced Sheet

The Mind(less) Muse: How She Does It; Loco-Motive

Muddy River Poetry Review: Aspen Grove; Grace;
        Lizard Karma

The New Moon Review: By the Roadside

Persimmon Tree: Cat Lives

Poetry Depth Quarterly: A Stranger's Horse

Continued next page

PUBLICATION CREDITS

Poetry Super Highway: Effigies

PoetryMagazine.com: Schaffung

Poets Online: St. Francis at the Door

Recursive Angel: A Venue, a Wake

Sacramento Voices: On a Wire

Schuylkill Valley Review: Holy Wells Day

Snapping Twig: Butterfly Effect; Shingle Creek

Song of the San Joaquin: Our Mouse

Spillway: Arrangements

Suisun Valley Review: Apogee

Tule Review: Alpenglow

Turtle Island Quarterly: Finding Me

Valparaiso Poetry Review: Talavera

Voices of Lincoln: Ten Years from Now

West Trestle Review: Shopping with Ginsberg

Wild: A Quarterly: Dog Poetry

Wilderness House Literary Review: Book of Hours; Uplift

Your Daily Poem: Caldera

"Diamondback" also appears in the chapbook
   Living with Myth (Rattlesnake Press), and
"Bird I Never Saw in Daylight" in the anthology
   Poeming Pigeons (The Poetry Box).